The Men Behind Moody

The Men Behind Moody

by
Robert G. Flood
and
Jerry B. Jenkins

MOODY PRESS
CHICAGO

© 1984 by
THE MOODY BIBLE INSTITUTE
OF CHICAGO

Library of Congress Cataloging in Publication Data

Flood, Robert G.
  The men behind Moody.

  1. Moody Bible Institute—History.   2. Moody Bible
Institute—Presidents—Biography.   I. Jenkins, Jerry B.
II. Title.
BV4070.M76F56   1984   207′.77311   84-20747
ISBN: 0-8024-5393-7 (pbk.)

  1 2 3 4 5 6 7 Printing/OP/Year 87 86 85 84

Printed in the United States of America

Contents

1

Dwight L. Moody, Evangelist

The sound of the woodchopper echoed through the trees in extreme northwest Massachusetts, within sight of New Hampshire and Vermont. The young boy on the end of the ax seemed to abound with energy.

He knew how to work. It took that kind of person to survive on those rocky New England farms, where someone once quipped that "there are sufficient stones to build four fences to the acre."

While Dwight Lyman Moody was a young boy, his father died, leaving nine sons and daughters. The oldest of the boys ran away. The broken-hearted widow, doubly bereft, began a heroic struggle against poverty.

Her little son Dwight grew up with scanty education but an unusually imaginative mind. Reminisced the *Chicago Tribune* on the centennial of his birth, "Moody received many maternal blisterings, for he was rather wild and wound up with tricks."[1]

The youngster delighted to play Indian and frighten fidgety Squire Alexander's cattle at night. In school he delivered Marc Antony's oration over Caesar and for effect used a miniature coffin containing a much alarmed tomcat as Caesar's corpse.

At seventeen, Moody went across the state to Boston, to work in his uncle's shoe store.

He turned out to be a first-class salesman. No shoddy pair of shoes walked past him without a challenge. Nor was he content to let prospects come to him. He stood out on the sidewalks and went after the crowds. You have to go where the people are, he believed.

At the persuasion of his uncle, Moody attended the Mount Vernon Congregational Church in Boston. There he sat under a Bible teacher named Edward Kimball. And Kimball followed up on his pupils. Concerned about Moody's soul, Kimball hastened to the shoe store one day and brought Moody right to the point. Jesus had died for him, Kimball pressed, and it was time for Moody to make a decision. The timing was right. Moody responded.

In time Moody's spiritual life began to blossom.

1. Frank Cipriani, "The Sinner Saver," *Chicago Tribune,* 24 January 1937.

Just as suddenly as he had left the hamlet of Northfield for Boston, Moody left Boston for Chicago, not telling his family. Upon his arrival in the fall of 1856, he dashed them off a quick note with the startling information, "God is the same here as in Boston."

A boot store promptly hired Moody and made him their traveling representative. The ambitious Moody immediately set his goal: a fortune of $100,000.

But shoes were no longer his only product. He also wanted to tell people about God. He rented a pew in Plymouth Church and went out onto the streets to fill it. He filled not only one pew, but four. Nor did he pick and choose his prospects. Everyone from beggars to business executives were eligible for a Moody approach:

"Are you a Christian?"

Unless the prospect could retort promptly with a convincing answer, he would find Moody in quick pursuit.

"Why not?"

Moody's reputation spread. One man handled Moody's stock question with, "That's none of your business."

"Oh, yes, it is," Moody snapped back.

The man eyed him warily.

"Then you must be Moody."

Moody's approach took courage. The streets were tough—vice flourished, temptations abounded. But Moody let nothing swerve him from his mission.

When he asked to teach a Bible class, he was told there was nothing open. He went out on the streets and recruited a class of his own, urchins of all sorts.

But Moody could relate also to the top ranks of Chicago's social class. As God is no respector of persons, Moody took men as they were.

As Moody's fame grew, journalists called him "Brother Moody." Some of the heretics in the street had a different name—"Crazy Moody." Bad press could not daunt him. Moody used the press to advertise and help fill his pews.

When Moody rode the streets on an Indian pony, handing out candy apples and rounding up kids for his Sunday school, critics wrote it off as a publicity stunt. But Moody drew attention to himself only because he wanted to bring all he could to the Savior.

As the work grew, Moody searched for larger quarters. He rented a large, grimy hall on North Market Street and promptly filled it with more than five hundred a Sunday. It was hardly the place you would want to host a dignitary, but word of Moody's success in the inner city reached Abraham Lincoln. The president-elect dropped in to see it for himself on his way from Springfield to Washington, D.C., for his inauguration.

Before Lincoln left, he told the crowded Sunday school class, "I was once as poor as any boy in this school, but I am now President of the United States, and if you attend to what is taught you here, some one of you may yet be President of the United States."[2]

Moody proved to be the primary catalyst for a movement that would soon become known as the Young Men's Christian Association (YMCA), of which he was president for a time.

By 1860 Moody was making a major impact on Chicago. During the war, he was an abolitionist and for the Union, but he could not bear to "shoot down a fellow human being." So in Chicago he conducted missionary services among the Union soldiers at Camp Douglas and later among some nine thousand Confederate prisoners, after the camp had been converted into a war prison.

But it had always been Moody's bent to go where the people were, and most soldiers were not in Chicago; they were on the front lines. Moody offered himself as a volunteer chaplain and headed south—to Shiloh, Murfreesboro, Chattanooga. He was the first to enter Richmond. He used the boom of his voice, not that of cannon, to mount his spiritual assault, and the Bible was his ammunition.

During the war Moody fell in love and in 1862 married Emma Revell, sister of publisher Fleming H. Revell, a name still prominent in Christian publishing. Though Emma was only fifteen, Moody had found a partner entirely in tune with

2. Ibid.

the call of God upon his life, one he saw as the "divinely appointed balance wheel of his existence."

Though his ministry at times took him far from home, Moody's tender letters home reflected his character as a family man. Emma, too, smoothed his rough edges and brought to the marriage a decidedly superior education.

Back in Chicago after the Civil War, two movements took much of Moody's attention: the YMCA and the spread of the Sunday school throughout the Midwest. On the former, he worked closely with merchant John V. Farwell and raised money to build the first "Y" hall in America. Cyrus McCormick, inventor of the reaper, gave Moody the first $10,000 for the project. It burned four months later, but before the embers had cooled, Moody had agents out raising funds to replace it.

Moody knew how to tap the well-to-do for funds, but it was not for his own welfare. It was for the welfare of others and the advance of the gospel. By now Moody had shifted his priorities and scuttled his ambition for wealth. He could have become a millionaire, said his close friends, but the Wall Street panic of 1857 convinced him he should not regard faith as primarily "an aid to fortune." Of his merchant associates in Chicago, Moody once said, "I felt I could equal any of them, except one—and that one was Marshall Field."[3]

3. Ibid.

As the number of Moody's converts grew, he realized he would have to build an edifice where spiritual growth could be nourished. So in 1864, with twelve charter members, Moody opened the Illinois Street Independent Church, with several classrooms and an auditorium seating fifteen hundred. The church called J. H. Harwood as its pastor, while Moody served as one of the deacons. It was the beginning of what would eventually become Moody Church.

In 1867 Emma Moody suffered from a chronic cough, and her doctor suggested a sea voyage. Moody took her to Great Britain, where they met George Mueller and Charles Spurgeon. When introduced to a London gathering as "their American cousin, the Reverend Mr. Moody of Chicago," Moody replied:

"The chairman has made two mistakes. To begin with, I'm not the 'Reverend' Mr. Moody at all. I'm plain D. L. Moody, a Sunday school worker. And then I'm not your 'American cousin.' By the grace of God I'm your brother, who is interested, with you, in our Father's work for His children." The crowd, accustomed to English formalities, found Moody's candidness refreshing. Six years later Moody would rock the British Isles with his first full-scale campaign.

An event that set the stage for several successful decades of ministry happened in Indianapolis at a convention of the Christian Association. There in 1870 Moody met Ira Sankey, an internal revenue collector who would become his famous soloist for the next quarter century.

The first time Moody heard Sankey's booming voice lead a morning prayer meeting in "There Is a Fountain Filled with Blood," he sought out Sankey after the meeting.

"I want you."

"What for?"

"To help me in my work in Chicago."

"But I can't leave my business."

"You must. I have been looking for you for eight years."[4]

The combination of the short, bearded evangelist and the tall, side-whiskered Sankey proved a spectacular success. One report called it "something like the words-and-music combination of Gilbert and Sullivan."

In Chicago, the crowds at Farwell Hall grew, and the Lord's work prospered. One Sunday evening in October 1871, as Moody was preaching, ominous flames erupted on Chicago's South Side. The story of Mrs. O'Leary's cow stands only as legend, but whatever sparked the blaze, by midnight the populace was fleeing in panic. The inferno swept northward block by block, reducing the city to ashes.

Moody had been preaching that evening on the text "What will you do with Jesus who is called the Christ?" Soloist Ira Sankey then sang, "Today the Saviour Calls."

4. Horace Thorogood, "Moody—Salesman of Salvation," *Evening Standard,* 4 February 1937.

Moody urged his audience to consider choosing Christ and to return the following Sunday to make a decision. But that night Farwell Hall, along with most of Chicago, burned to the ground and three hundred people died.

From that time forward, Moody vowed he would press the decision for salvation *now*, not sometime later.

As the courthouse bell rang out the alarm and the first horse-drawn fire engines rushed toward the scene, Moody had to dismiss the capacity crowd. Hundreds in the gathering hurried to aid their families or others.

As Moody made his way toward his own home, hurricane-like southwest winds from the fire blew sparks down around him, touching off first one house, then another. "The city's doomed," he told Emma as he arrived at home.

The Moodys thought their own home perhaps far enough from the blaze to escape, but in the early morning hours police urged a fast getaway. Dwight and Emma dispatched their two children to the suburbs with a neighbor and began gathering a few belongings.

Among them happened to be a cherished portrait of D. L. Moody by G. P. A. Healy, the most famous portrait artist of that day. Healy had given it to Moody upon his return from his family vacation in Great Britain. Emma urged Moody to save the painting.

"Take my own picture?" He laughed. "That would be a joke. Suppose I meet some friends in the same trouble as ourselves and they say, "Hullo, Moody, glad you have escaped. What's that you've saved and cling to so affectionately?' "

Looters already on the scene obligingly cut it out of its frame and handed it to his wife.

The great Chicago fire destroyed Moody's lovely home, which had been provided and furnished by friends less than a year earlier. The harrowing experience turned Mrs. Moody, then just twenty-eight, gray almost overnight.

The fire destroyed also the YMCA and Moody's church. While he was greatly disappointed, in Moody's eyes it was not the worst catastrophe that could happen to man. It was far worse that anyone should not hear clearly the gospel. The Chicago fire impressed upon him a new urgency.

With his typical endless energy, Moody sprang into action. He rebuilt his church within a few weeks, named his new building the North Side Tabernacle, and turned it into a relief center to help feed and clothe the thousands who had lost their homes in the fire.

While in New York City raising money to rebuild, Moody's heart was set aflame. As he walked along a street in New York City, he received the answer to his prayer for a special infilling of the Holy Spirit.

"I was crying all the time that God would fill me with His Spirit. Well, one day in the city of New York—O what a day! I cannot describe it. I seldom refer to it. It is almost too sacred an experience to name. I can only say God revealed Himself to me, and I had such an experience of His love that I had to ask Him to stay His hand! I went to preaching again. The sermons were not different, yet hundreds were converted."[5]

The Moody-Sankey Great Britain campaign got its first spark from a spur-of-the-moment invitation. Moody was invited to speak in a London church. At the close he asked those who wanted "to have [their] lives changed by the power of God through faith in Jesus Christ as a personal Saviour" and who "wanted to become Christians" to rise. People rose everywhere.

Moody thought they had misunderstood and tried to clarify his invitation. Scores still came forward as Moody and the host minister looked on, astonished. The phenomenon repeated itself the next night. Moody returned to the States and laid plans for a full-fledged campaign the next year.

That campaign got off to an uncertain start in June 1873. Little seemed to happen at first—at least on the surface. Britons were not used to Moody's informal preaching style or to Sankey's portable organ. They winced at the American evangelist's accent and his sometimes poor English, but the spirit of God began to work.

Sankey's music caught hold. Crowds grew. The campaign extended into weeks, then months.

5. Alfred Bal, "The Man Who Spoke to 100,000,000," *Sunday Digest*, 24 July 1960.

Stores by the thousands displayed revival posters. Government leaders, including British Prime Minister William Gladstone, complimented and endorsed Moody. Communists denounced his work as a "bourgeois plot to import intellectual opium."[6]

Moody and Sankey moved on to Scotland, where antiritualistic Scots at first raised their eyebrows at Sankey's organ and criticized Moody's grammar. But revival soon took hold. Moody drew tremendous gatherings in Glasgow. When an auditorium overflowed, he addressed an estimated 50,000 outside from a buggy. He later moved on to Ireland, touching Belfast, Londonderry, and other cities and winning friendly words from the leading Irish Catholic newspapers.

Then he took on London. By the time he left the British Isles, Moody had spoken to 2.5 million.

The impact of the campaign would be felt throughout England for decades. It had started with England's middle class, spread to the poor, and eventually permeated even the aristocracy, including the Princess of Wales. When the campaign closed after two years, all Great Britain was talking about Moody and Sankey. They returned to America as world-famous figures.

The Moody-Sankey hymnals introduced in the campaign sold like hotcakes in Great Britain and

6. Cipriani, "The Sinner Saver."

America as well. Royalties began to pile up, leading to rumors that Moody and Sankey were growing rich on them and that P. T. Barnum, the circus magnate, was backing them.

Moody sent the first British royalties, totaling $35,000, home to Chicago to complete his newest church at Chicago Avenue and LaSalle. By the turn of the century the Moody-Sankey hymnal had generated well over $1 million in royalties, but it was all channeled into evangelistic and philanthropic causes. Moody and Sankey made not a penny of personal profit.

Neither Moody nor Sankey let the success of the British Isles campaign spoil them. They clearly understood the source of the spiritual power that had swept Great Britain. And if it could happen there, it could also happen in America. Moody began to outline an American revival. The nation needed it. The Civil War, like all wars, had disrupted general morality. People chased after easy wealth. Corruption penetrated high political office.

Target cities were New York, Brooklyn, and Philadelphia—with Brooklyn the opener in October 1875. Rich and poor alike poured in, though the press gave mixed reviews. Although some ridiculed Moody's grammar, the *New York Tribune* said, "Christianity is not a matter of grammar." And thousands came to Christ.

It was a similar story in Philadelphia. Merchant John Wanamaker let Moody preach in the old freight depot of the Pennsylvania railroad, which Wanamaker had purchased and would later make into a store. One evening President Grant and several of his cabinet sat on the platform.

Then followed great campaigns in New York, Chicago, Boston, Baltimore, Cleveland, Cincinnati, Richmond, Denver, Colorado Springs, St. Louis, San Francisco. Canada and Mexico also wanted him, but his schedule would not permit it.*

Moody's British and American campaigns, demanding as they were, still seemed to leave him time for other Christian pursuits. Among them were schools he established at Northfield, his birthplace. In 1879, nearly a decade before Moody Bible Institute would become a reality, he opened the Northfield Seminary for Young Women. Two years later in the same town he started the Mount Hermon School for Young Men. These high schools offered a practical curriculum, with the Bible at the center. Later Northfield became the scene of great summer conferences—the largest of their kind in the world.

*Moody preached not only in the big cities but also in many smaller towns across the nation. Should you want to know, out of curiosity, if and when Dwight L. Moody ever came to your town, the Moody Bible Institute librarian can tell you to the day. And he may even be able to come up with a newspaper clipping of what Moody said that day. The Institute's Moodyana collection includes over 1,200 of Moody's letters in nine bound volumes, indexed and arranged chronologically. From these letters and other sources, the library has compiled a chronological summary of Moody's life, detailing where he was and what he did on almost every day between 1834 and 1899.

Moody went abroad again for another British revival in 1881. It was every bit as great as the first one, and again the city of London gave him a great reception. During the campaign he spoke to 2 million persons. A third campaign followed.

P. W. Philpott, late pastor of Moody Memorial Church, wrote in *The Chicago Tribune,* "Moody's three triumphant tours of Great Britain had a tremendous influence in drawing England and America closer together."

2

Moody's Chicago School

Dwight L. Moody's dream of a school in Chicago simmered on a back burner for nearly two decades before 1886. That year Moody met with a group in his room at the Grand Pacific Hotel in Chicago. A constitution for the "Chicago Evangelization Society" had been drafted, and at the meeting a committee was appointed to secure a charter. That became the official first document, or birth certificate, of what later became the Moody Bible Institute.

Six highly qualified men were appointed as trustees:

Nathaniel S. Bouton, one of the West's most prominent producers of architectural iron and railway castings. As Chicago's former Superintendent of Public Works, his administration had given Chicago its first paved streets.

John V. Farwell, one of Chicago's most prominent dry goods merchants (his firm would be bought out by Carson, Pirie, Scott & Company in 1925). Farwell was also vice-president of the Chicago Board of Trade, presidential elector on the Lincoln ticket in 1860, and later Indian Commissioner under President Ulysses S. Grant. Moody and Farwell were such close friends that someone once called Farwell "the inventor of Dwight L. Moody." "I didn't create him," Farwell countered, "God did."

T. W. Harvey, one of Chicago's pioneer lumbermen and at one time the greatest retail lumber dealer in the world. In Michigan, Harvey built the first logging railroad ever constructed. He also founded the town of Harvey, twenty miles south of Chicago's Loop.

Elbridge G. Keith, one of the organizers and president of Chicago's Metropolitan National Bank, and later president of the Chicago Title and Trust Company. Keith served as Moody Bible Institute's treasurer for eighteen years.

Cyrus H. McCormick, Jr., son of the inventor of the reaper. McCormick was president, chairman of the board, and executive of the International Harvester Company for thirty-three years. One of the wealthiest men in the country, he built the present Chicago YWCA building on North Dearborn in memory of his wife, served on a diplomatic mission to Russia, was a trustee of Princeton University, and served as director of McCormick Theological Seminary.

Robert S. Scott, senior partner in what is now

Carson, Pirie, Scott, and Company, still one of Chicago's foremost department stores.

The Chicago Evangelization Society absorbed a city outreach that had been established some years earlier by Emma Dryer, an Illinois educator who had helped Moody in his relief work following the Chicago fire. Moody's school, in fact, had been in part her vision and initiative. It had also been encouraged by the Cyrus McCormicks, strong supporters of both Dwight Moody and the work of Emma Dryer.

The Chicago Evangelization Society began to reach out to the city in tent meetings, thousands of home calls, Bible classes, and the like. But there were growing pains. It was a pioneer work with no previous pattern.

Importing theological talent, Emma Dryer had also established an annual month-long biblical "institute" held in Chicago each May. But the Chicago Evangelization Society still had not developed into a full-time school. Nor did it have its own building or resident campus.

One evening John Morrison, an usher in Moody's Chicago Avenue Church, stepped outside the church's northwest door for a breath of air.

"Is that you, Morrison?" asked Moody, who was to preach that night. "Do you see that lot? Let us pray the Lord to give it to us for a school."

The two men knelt and prayed right there.

In their wildest imaginations, the two men could not have envisioned how God would answer that prayer, nor the vast complex that would stand on that very lot and surrounding properties a century later.

In September 1889, Moody hustled back from a campaign in San Francisco to push his Chicago school. Enthusiasm ran high. The board moved quickly to buy the three houses next to the Chicago Avenue Church, and the lot for which Moody and Morrison had prayed. The existing structures were remodeled, and construction began on a three-story men's dormitory and main office building at 80 West Pearson Street. A few years later, when Chicago introduced its new street-numbering system, the structure became 153 Institute Place—the building that named a street. The building would become known around the world, and in actuality it would mark the beginning of the entire Bible institute movement.

Moody himself was the school's president, but he could not administer its day-by-day operation. Moody selected as superintendent the brilliant, young Dr. Reuben A. Torrey, graduate of Yale College and Seminary, who had also studied abroad. Torrey had his first taste of soul-winning in Moody's great New Haven campaign on the threshhold of Yale University.

At the dedication of the 153 Building on January 16, 1890, Moody outlined the purpose of the school—to train men and women for city visitation and foreign missions and to train both evangelists and musicians.

The 1893 Chicago World's Fair (Columbian Exposition) gave Moody and his Bible institute the perfect arena for putting evangelism into action. Despite doctor's warnings to slow down, Moody planned the largest single campaign of his career.

Two floors were added to the 153 Building to accommodate visitors and the increasing enrollment that Moody anticipated the fair would bring. The city's evangelical forces mobilized behind him, with the Moody "campus"—such as it was—his campaign headquarters. Clinics on evangelism were set up in eighty churches, tents, theaters, missions, and halls throughout Chicago. Foreign language interpreters were recruited.

By the time the fair was over, Moody's meetings at the exposition had drawn nearly 2 million people.

The school grew and prospered spiritually. Benefactors like Cyrus McCormick saw that it had needed funds. Moody constantly scoured the horizons for good Bible teachers, and his contacts were many. By the turn of the century, an almost constant stream of figures from the world's evangelical *Who's Who* had preached and taught on campus. These included F. B. Meyer and G. Campbell Morgan of London, Andrew Murray of South Africa, C. I. Scofield of Dallas, China missionary J. Hudson Taylor, and many others.

Even then many called the school "Moody's," as some today do. Yet it was not officially named

Moody Bible Institute until after the evangelist's death. Moody would not have allowed it.

Dwight Moody founded not only a school but a publishing firm. After a series of meetings in Madison, Wisconsin, in 1894, Moody looked around for a booklet on Christian growth that he could leave with his new converts. He found none. He continued to search for Christian books in the cities in which he preached, but with little success. Dime novels were the rage, and people eagerly read books about Jesse James and Diamond Dick.

Moody urged several Christian publishers to publish inexpensive Christian literature on a mass basis, but all were reluctant to take the risk in the absence of general demand. So he decided to do it himself. In November of 1894, he formed the Bible Institute Colportage Association of Chicago, forerunner of Moody Press. Dwight L. Moody introduced the inexpensive religious paperback decades before the paperback became standard in the book world.

The press runs of those early years were large. The first edition of *The Way to God*, by Moody, totaled 100,000. *All of Grace*, by Charles Spurgeon also sold in high volume. "If we believe the gospel is the best news that ever came to the world," Moody once said, "then let us publish it to everybody we can reach."

The school prospered, but on December 22, 1899, newspaper headlines across the nation and even abroad shouted the news that Moody had died while in the midst of a campaign in Kansas City. His followers reeled in shock.

Moody had changed the moral tone of two continents. In a tribute to him at his death, the *Chicago Times Herald* wrote: "Moody found that the sacrificial atonement of the Nazarene had power to touch the hearts of men, and he preached it as Paul preached it in Syria and Macedonia, without embellishment or studied rhetoric. He left the battle of the creeds to be waged by the cloistered scholars. His profession was not theology. He was about his Master's business. While theologians emptied pews with dogmatic controversy, Moody filled great auditoriums with the masses of the people who were hungry for the simple consolations of religion.[1]

When Moody's life ended, America, Europe— the world—mourned. God had used him to change millions of lives and to leave a spiritual legacy that continues to impact the world. The stocky man with broad shoulders left his indelible imprint upon a major Midwest city. Chicago at one time claimed this mighty preacher, but by the time he died the whole world claimed him.

On a chilly day in December, just before the turn of the century, D. L. Moody was buried on the top of a round knoll only a couple of hundred

---

1. "Dwight L. Moody" obituary, *Chicago Times Herald*, 23 December 1899.

yards from his Northfield birthplace. In those intervening sixty-five years, Moody had traveled a million miles for the sake of his Savior and had preached to 100 million people.

He brought God to men, and men to God.

3

The Torrey Years

The opening days of the twentieth century were the perfect time for a new run at the future. But only a week earlier the one who so admirably inspired "shoeleather evangelism" had suddenly passed from the scene. Quaker Oats executive Henry Parsons Crowell said that when Moody died, "it seemed as if the life had gone out of the Institute."[1] Superintendent R. A. Torrey, however, gave assurance that the work would go on.

Could the school Moody founded take on the new century without him? Would those who had so earnestly supported it still do so without Moody on the scene? And what directions would it take?

"The monument I want when I am dead and

1. Dorothy Martin, *God's Power in Action* (Chicago: Moody, 1977), p. 40.

31

gone," Moody had once said, "is a monument on two legs going about the world."[2]

Many also wondered if the Institute could stand true to its biblical doctrines as the winds of theological controversy blew across the land.

R. A. Torrey soon proved himself the right man for the times.

Though raised in a godly home, Torrey had by college days acquired only a veneer of Christianity. At Yale he buckled under social pressure and became a heavy drinker. In his senior year, however, he found personal salvation. When Moody came to town, Torrey involved himself in the crusade.

Torrey's conversion, however, had not settled all his intellectual doubts—even as he pursued theological studies at Yale Seminary. "The professors were all orthodox," Torrey said, "but I was not."[3]

Could he really believe in the resurrection, as told in the Scriptures? Torrey dug into the evidence in depth and found it overwhelming. "That conclusion," he said, "carried everything with it that was essential."[4]

But Torrey had also followed the transcendental thinkers and read heavily in Unitarianism. Questions remained. From Yale, Torrey pursued studies in Leipzig and Erlangen, Germany, and faced head-on the arguments of the "higher crit-

2. Ibid.
3. Ibid., p. 41.
4. Ibid.

ics." Abroad he settled the question once and for all. Yes, he could trust the Bible, its infallibility, its full authority. And he knew why. Torrey never wavered again.

On return from Germany, Torrey became superintendent of a city mission in Minneapolis. He gave up his salary and deliberately put himself out on a financial limb. City work gave him further seasoning and exposed him to the gospel's power in the lives of men. Such background produced a man who could handle himself and the Scriptures well, whether on skid row or among theological scholars. Said one biographer, "He could kneel beside a drunk in a mission or explain the gospel at an elegant dinner table."[5]

It was this combination that gave Dwight L. Moody's successor the credentials to formulate a solid school curriculum and answer the arguments of the higher critics, while at the same time enthusiastically directing the school's city outreach.

Torrey perceived well what he needed to do with the Institute. Moody had relied heavily on guest teachers. Torrey saw the danger that students might look more to prominent men than to the Scriptures themselves. The school needed a resident faculty and a curriculum with more continuity. Guest teachers often differed in certain details of doctrinal viewpoint.

In its aggressive outreach to the city, the Insti-

5. Ibid., p. 44.

tute originated, under Torrey, what became known as the "gospel wagon." These horse-pulled wagons each held a small organ, a desk for a pulpit, and a few seats for a choir. It was designed to "go where the people were." Within a few years, as Moody graduates dispersed abroad, the gospel wagon could even be seen across Europe.

Others besides Reuben Torrey helped shape the Institute in those early years.

Shortly after Moody's death, his only son-in-law, A. P. Fitt, was elected to the board (for a short while he even held the title of president). Fitt handled executive duties in the transition period. He proved an excellent liaison with Moody's friends around the world and also between Chicago and the Northfield schools, which had been entrusted to Moody's oldest son, Will.

More prominent names were added to the board. Publisher Fleming H. Revell, Moody's brother-in-law, became a trustee in 1900. Among others who later joined were world-famous gynecologist Dr. Howard A. Kelly of Baltimore and William Whiting Borden, wealthy New England heir immortalized in missionary annals as "Borden of Yale."

Then there was Thomas S. Smith, "apple king of the Midwest." He had walked forward in the Chicago Avenue church one night when D. L. Moody was preaching. Moody took his hand, looked in his face, and said, "Young man, God has a place for you!"

Thomas Smith served on the Moody Bible Institute board for forty-three years, twenty as vice-chairman. Quiet and unassuming, he arose every morning at 4:00 A.M. for his quiet time before going to the old South Water Street market. His son, Wilbur M. Smith, became a Moody professor, noted Christian author, and long-time *Moody Monthly* magazine columnist.

James H. Todd was named the first superintendent of men. A. F. Gaylord, a student in 1891, became business manager that same year and held the job for forty-four years.

Henry Parsons Crowell, founder of Quaker Oats, stepped into the Institute scene in those early transitional years and helped chart its future. Crowell had never met Moody, but he had heard him preach once. The Chicago business executive lived on Rush Street, only a few blocks from the Institute, and was active at nearby Fourth Presbyterian Church on north Michigan Avenue. A godly man, it was no surprise that he should become interested in the work of the Moody Bible Institute.

Crowell and his wife invited Moody Bible teacher William R. Newell (author of the famous gospel song "At Calvary") into their home to conduct a weekly Bible class. The experience revolutionized their lives.

Crowell was elected to the board of trustees in

35

1901 and became president three years later—a position he would hold for forty years. As a hard-working trustee with keen business acumen, Crowell poured himself into the challenge, heart and soul.

As Crowell got close to the inner workings of the organization, he realized the school lacked a broad financial support base. D. L. Moody had relied heavily on the gifts of well-to-do business-men. Crowell envisioned thousands of donors across the country, who would give to the school on a regular basis, even if in small amounts. And with a broad financial base, the Institute would also have a broad prayer base. He theorized that people would pray more for the success of a pro-ject if their money was in it.

With godly wisdom and concern, Crowell saw another aspect. A broad base of support would help hold the school to its purpose, its biblical doctrine, its evangelical zeal. An expanded board of trustees also helped solidify the organization in transition. And Henry Crowell set for the Insti-tute a high standard of business ethics. No build-ing would be built, for example, until all the funds were in hand.

When the Institute set its course at the outset of the century, it put gospel music high in the curriculum. Though Moody himself could not carry a tune, he recognized music as a powerful medium for the gospel—a medium men could put either into the hands of God or into the hands of Satan. He used it well in his own crusades. Soloist Ira Sankey's health did not hold long enough for him to remain with Moody in latter years. But Hugh McGranahan, nephew of then famous composer James McGranahan, was tapped to head Moody Bible Institute's first music department. A rich heritage of gospel music blossomed as the years passed.

Reuben A. Torrey kept a close eye on student life when he was on campus, but Torrey was away on evangelistic campaigns much of the time. After nearly a decade as president, he resigned in 1909 for full-time evangelism. The crusades of R. A. Torrey brought further millions under the sound of the gospel during his career—with the impact upon Australia as great as upon any continent. In 1912 Torrey became dean of the Bible Institute of Los Angeles (now Biola University), where he served until 1924.

When Torrey left in 1909, the mantel fell on James M. Gray, who would guide Moody Bible Institute until it was almost a half century old.

4
The James M. Gray Years

Naught have I gotten but what I received;
Grace hath bestowed it since I have believed;
Boasting excluded, pride I abase;
I'm only a sinner saved by grace.

The words of "Only a Sinner" came from the pen of James M. Gray. They reflect the spirit of the man who would lead Moody Bible Institute through perilous times, early financial crisis, upheaval of world war, theological confusion, and the collapse of Wall Street.

For more than a quarter century Gray commanded the ship skillfully through rough waters. Yet it could hardly be said that he fit the image of a man who had ambitiously pushed himself up into the executive ranks.

And that may have been one reason for his success: he was completely uninterested in pushing himself.

"Whom am I serving?" he often asked.[1]

Gray was born in New York City in 1851 and converted as a young man. In 1879, at twenty-eight, he was called to the First Reformed Episcopal Church in Boston. There he pastored for twenty-five years and also taught Bible courses at what is now Gordon College.

Though a specialist in Bible exposition, Gray also set a fast pace in community affairs. At that time the major issue was anti-liquor legislation. Because Gray believed preaching against sin also meant taking action in the marketplace, he became an ardent prohibitionist.

As a student in New York, Gray sang in Moody's meetings at the Hippodrome and heard him preach many times. When Moody asked him to speak at his Northfield summer conference, Gray made the book of Job come alive to laymen. Moody was so impressed that he invited him to teach at the Institute during summer months. In fact, he put Gray in charge of the total operation while Torrey was away for four months on an evangelistic campaign.

By 1904 the Institute was still groping for a plan that would solve the dilemma of its day-to-day leadership, especially during Torrey's frequent absences. Henry Parsons Crowell urged that Gray accept the position of full-time dean. Gray was reluctant. But Crowell's gentle persuasion prevailed.

1. Dorothy Martin, *God's Power in Action* (Chicago: Moody, 1977), p. 66.

Technically, Gray did not become president of Moody Bible Institute until 1923, for until that time Henry Crowell, as chairman of the Executive Committee, carried that title. But in reality, Gray served in a presidential role.

The man who did not really want the top job not only demonstrated his administrative expertise, but he also proved a strong spokesman for biblical orthodoxy.

Although the era of Dwight L. Moody had its own doubters and skeptics, the drift from orthodoxy intensified after the turn of the century. Gray's abilities as a superb Bible teacher and expositor stood him well in the role of Christian apologist and defender of the faith.

Gray also employed the tools of a Christian journalist. During his years in Boston, he had seen firsthand the hold of Christian Science on sincere, earnest people. So he wrote *The Antidote to Christian Science*. He attacked not the people but the belief.

With Harry Emerson Fosdick, though, it was a different story. Fosdick had denied the faith he was ordained to uphold, and his book *The Peril of Worshipping Jesus* had documented his apostasy. Gray published a scalding reply in his own book *The Audacity of Unbelief*. Among Gray's other books in defense of the faith were *Why I Believe the Bible Will Stand, Why a Christian Cannot Be an Evolutionist,* and *Modernism, a Foe to Good Government*.

A strong push for an "interchurch world movement" emerged after World War I. Gray spoke out for denominations and the role of the local church. The Moody Bible Institute had always been interdenominational, and it would back those local churches who still stood for the fundamentals of the faith.

The term *fundamentalism* itself, of course, did not originate until shortly after 1909, when orthodox scholars released *The Fundamentals*, a defense of historic biblical doctrines. Over the years the Institute has held, without compromise, to the fundamental doctrines of evangelicalism.

Although James M. Gray defended the faith without compromise, he did so as a gentleman. It would have contradicted his quiet, dignified nature to do otherwise. Yet his words struck with power.

In 1914, with the world on the brink of World War I, the Institute sponsored a historic Prophetic Bible Conference at Moody Church to reaffirm the doctrines of historic Christianity, both for the church at large and for the Institute itself. Ministers gathered from across the country and went home feeling its great impact.

Gray was a Bible scholar, but he also knew how to make what he taught—and what he wrote—very clear. It was Gray who introduced the "synthetic" method of Bible study, which helped students see the Bible as a whole and each Bible book as a whole. His *How to Master the English Bible* became a classic. Other Bible institutes, colleges, and seminaries throughout the world picked up his method.

R. A. Torrey had already pioneered a study-by-mail program, and Gray's synthetic Bible study approach gave the fledgling Moody Correspondence School a boost. Moody Bible Institute quickly added correspondence courses in introductory Bible, Christian evidences, and evangelism. Close on the heels of those came Dr. C. I. Scofield's three-volume course, which covered the entire Bible.

Meanwhile, the Evening School also grew. At one point its curriculum duplicated the day school's, but it soon became impossible to crowd all of those courses into evening hours. Evening School was forced back into its original format and purpose—to train laymen in local churches, not necessarily full-time Christian workers.

The Institute chose for its spiritual motto 2 Timothy 2:15, "Study to show thyself approved unto God, a workman that needeth not to be ashamed, rightly dividing the word of truth."

Not only did MBI weather the fundamental-liberal storm and save its own destiny, it molded opinion as well. Wrote Jasper Mossee in *The World Book* in 1923, "In my judgment, the constituency that has gone out from the Moody Bible Institute during the last ten years has saved the evangelical churches of the country.[2]

Gray built and maintained a faculty that was

2. Rollin Lynde Hart, "The War in the Churches," *The World Book Encyclopedia*, September 1923, p. 472.

equally committed to the Scriptures. One of those he recruited was P. B. Fitzwater, who at one time was the most widely read newspaper writer in the world, having a syndicated column in 2,600 papers across the nation. Fitzwater, an able Bible scholar, served as dean and then director of the general course and the pastors' course for more than thirty years until his retirement in 1954. The main classroom building on campus bears his name.

Gray insisted that his faculty live near enough to the campus to be present at Institute functions. He wanted a close family atmosphere and a close management team.

In 1905 Gray combined the men's and women's departments, which had been separate. But men and women still continued to sit on separate sides in class—and in the dining room.

He also added English to the curriculum, which until this point had been a feature only of the evening school—to accommodate immigrants and help them understand the Bible.

From the school's outset, entrance requirements had been minimal. In Moody's day many people, though intelligent and self-educated, had not pursued formal study beyond the fifth or sixth grade. Now times were changing. Secular educators set higher standards. Gray insisted that minimal entrance requirements did not mean inferior education. But to move with the times, he proposed requiring a high school education for entrance.

The move triggered a storm of protest. Even Torrey feared this would keep out many for whom the school was originally intended. But the move was made anyway, and the storm eventually subsided.

The earliest days of Gray's regime saw little monies to expand the campus. But after a time the Institute acquired adjacent properties and in 1909 it built an additional men's dormitory (152 Institute Place), formally renamed Norton Hall in 1951. Nearly two decades later, the building—which stood approximately where the underground student dining hall is today—was torn down to develop the new campus. (In the early seventies the "Norton" name was transferred to a newly-acquired building near the Chicago suburb of Evanston.)

In 1912, the Women's Building (830 N. LaSalle) arose. Now Smith Hall, it houses offices on the first three floors, and students on the upper floors. The building has been so modernized that it is now difficult to tell that it was one of the school's earliest buildings.

The old Moody Church on the corner of La-Salle and Chicago was the Institute's next major purchase. It became the school's auditorium. The Moody Church congregation in 1915 built a 5,000-seat tabernacle, with sawdust floor, on North Avenue, and then dedicated its present 4,200-seat edifice in 1925.

James M. Gray gave Moody Bible Institute its school song in 1909, with music professor D. B.

Towner supplying the tune. In years to come it would become loved by thousands all over the world. Gray wrote many other hymns and gospel songs, some of which remain standards in American hymnals.

Others of the Moody Bible Institute also contributed. T. J. Bitikofer wrote "Complete in Thee." E. O. Sellers wrote "Wonderful, Wonderful Jesus." William M. Runyan wrote the music to "Great Is Thy Faithfulness." George C. Stebbins originated the music for "Jesus Is Calling" and "Take Time to Be Holy." Al Smith wrote "My Father Planned It All." Merrill Dunlop wrote the music to "Only One Life."

Moody Bible Institute came into existence during a period when the gospel song had just emerged. The Moody-Sankey campaigns popularized it. Most of these songs had an evangelistic text, a tuneful melody, a catchy rhythm, and simple harmony. As Moody was the key evangelist of his time, it should have been no surprise that the school he founded would shape church music for decades.

In the mid twenties the nation had begun to pioneer a new medium called radio. Henry Coleman Crowell, son of the Quaker Oats founder, had just joined the Moody staff. With the foresight characteristic of his father, he realized radio's potential.

Gray at first did not think Christians had any business tampering with the air waves because Scripture defines Satan as "prince of the power of the air." Along with some other Christians of his day, he saw it as a potentially dangerous realm, though he had other reservations as well. Their misgivings may leave us amused, but even Gray shortly changed his mind. When in 1926 a North Dakota resident wrote to Moody Bible Institute and asked, "Is radio of God or the devil?" President Gray answered, "We think it is of God."[3]

Moody Bible Institute went on the air that same year with one of the first religious broadcasts in the nation. Calvin Coolidge was in the White House. The Scopes "Monkey trial" was a year past. Charles Lindbergh's flight to Paris was a year ahead. It was the midpoint of the Roaring Twenties; the era of twenty-dollar rent, the five-cent trolly, and "listening in."

The Institute took its first step into radio when it bought a used 500-watt transmitter from the *Detroit Daily News* and installed it in a tiny penthouse atop what is now Smith Hall. For a studio, it hung the ground floor of a men's dormitory with heavy drapes. The Institute applied for a license, but there seemed little hope in the chaotic scramble with the government for wavelengths.

On July 27, 1926, a wire arrived from Washington. An unexpected shift had opened up a frequency, the only one in Chicago. The Institute

3. James M. Gray, "Radio," *Moody Bible Institute Monthly*, March 1926, p. 309.

could launch a station, WMBI, if it could move in quickly. WMBI went on the air the next day. Gray, still a bit skeptical, delivered a gospel message. After the broadcast, he walked out of the studio, proceeded across Institute Place, and stepped into his office. The phone rang. To Gary's astonishment, it was a call from Florida, reporting that his message had just been received there. More calls and letters followed. Gray's doubts about radio were soon dispelled.

Gray encouraged the work of the Bible Institute Colportage Association and laid the foundations of what later became *Moody Monthly* magazine. When in 1907 Gray and Torrey took over as coeditors of the old *Institute Tie,* they immediately altered its format to more of an educational one, in order to reach out beyond MBI's alumni and close circle of friends. It was a wise first step toward the much broader market the magazine would later enjoy.

When James M. Gray retired from the presidency in 1934, depression still lay heavy across the land. A year earlier, in an attempt to bolster spirits, Chicago had staged its 1933 "Century of Progress" Exposition. But it was a bit like whistling in the dark. Gloom prevailed. Moody Bible Institute felt the economic impact of the time, but its own mission, its spirit, its vigor, stood above temporal events. Moody's graduates continued to stream into the nation's pulpits and into a broad cross-section of other Christian ministries. And they continued to sail to the mission fields of the world.

Already MBI was almost fifty years old, and some of its graduates had already spent a good portion of their lives in Christian service at home or abroad. The rich heritage that Moody, Torrey, Gray, their associates, and the school's alumni had already passed on would lay the foundations of the next half century.

5

The Houghton Years

Young Will Houghton had a natural talent for the stage. In his teens, and against his mother's objections, he signed with a touring company. He developed into a seasoned vaudeville actor, circuiting the country with his own comedy act.

His theatrical career came to an abrupt end at age twenty-three when a sermon in his mother's church brought him under conviction. Though he had already received Christ during an evangelistic crusade at fourteen, Houghton now surrendered all. He abandoned the stage.

After further education, Houghton launched into the ministry, gaining practical on-the-job experience with itinerant evangelists in the New York area. He became a songleader, gospel singer, and budding preacher. He eventually came to the attention of Reuben A. Torrey, who saw great potential in the young man and took him under

51

his tutelage. When Houghton took his first church, nine people were converted at his trial sermon, the first of thousands. Large crowds turned out to hear his most popular sermon, "From Stage to Pulpit."[1]

Adelaide, Houghton's wife of two years, took suddenly ill in the summer of 1916 and died that autumn, leaving him with two infants. Two years later Houghton married Elizabeth Andrews, whom he had met while serving as a chaplain to World War I troops leaving for the front lines.

God's hand seemed to be upon all that Houghton undertook. He pastored a church near Philadelphia with stunning results. After preaching to great crowds in Ireland, he accepted a call to the Baptist Tabernacle in Atlanta, one of the South's most influential congregations. Three years later he left that church at its peak attendance of 4,000 to pastor the Calvary Baptist Church of New York City, a block from Carnegie Hall.

There Will Houghton—evangelist, church builder, and Bible teacher—had to follow John Roach Stratton. Church attendance had plummeted upon Pastor Stratton's death. Calvary's new skyscraper church/hotel complex stood half completed when the stock market crashed.

Houghton rebuilt the congregation, and saw completion of the new auditorium, embedded

1. William R. DePlata, *Tell It from Calvary* (Calvary Baptist Church: New York, 1972), p. 59.

inside the church's 320-room Hotel Salisbury. Houghton found himself in the role of pastor and hotel president. He filled both the church and the hotel.

Crowds packed Calvary's downtown Manhattan church on Friday nights for youth rallies that foreshadowed the Youth For Christ movement still a decade or two away. Calvary's radio outreach sent both Houghton's sermons and his melodious baritone voice out across New York City.

Now into his eighties, James M. Gray decided to retire as MBI president and handpick his successor. Neither the board nor Gray could seem to find just the right man. Then in early 1934 Gray chaired a Moody-sponsored Bible conference in Calvary Baptist Church. At the Sunday morning service he heard Dr. Will Houghton preach. Immediately Gray decided, "There is the man to follow me at the Institute."[2]

For Houghton it was another call to the city, this time the "city with broad shoulders." It was also a call to the pulpit, a call to the Word of God he loved so well, a call to young people, to radio, to writing—all of which Houghton had handled well. And his experience in the building program in New York City brought further expertise into his new role.

Moody Bible Institute now had over 900 students, a radio station, a correspondence school, a magazine, and a book publishing operation.

2. Ibid., p. 65.

Houghton characterized himself as a "creator of ideas." But he knew the future dare not be built on mere human ingenuity. His first move was to call the Institute to prayer, including its alumni around the world. "God alone," he said, "is equal to the needs."[3]

Only a month after Houghton's inauguration, the martyrdom of MBI graduates John and Betty Stam in China shocked the Christian world. On December 7, 1934, Communists had looted their mission station at Tsingteh, Anhwei Province, taken them hostage, and demanded $20,000 ransom. The next day, before negotiations could be completed, their decapitated bodies were found along the road.

At the news of the tragedy, many offered their lives to spread the gospel abroad. In memory of the Stams, Will Houghton wrote a poem, "By Life o By Death," later set to music by George S. Schuler.

Houghton was a master promoter, and the Institute needed all it could get to keep its head above water in the rough seas of economic depression. Two events gave Houghton the ideal occasion: the fiftieth anniversary of the Institute and the centennial of Moody's birth. He called for a massive two-year celebration, with a strong evangelistic emphasis.

The Institute pushed plans to observe the two

3. Dorothy Martin, *God's Power in Action* (Chicago: Moody, 1977), p. 100.

events both in the United States and in Great Britain, the scene of Moody's greatest evangelistic campaigns. Churches in every state and thirty foreign countries observed "Moody Day," Sunday, February 7, 1937. Twelve thousand crowded the Chicago Coliseum on February 5, Moody's birth date. Secular magazines and newspapers as well as Christian publications rehearsed his life and work. Newspapers like the *Chicago Tribune* and the *New York Times* gave it a page or more. Even the ultraliberal *Christian Century* paid Moody a two-page editorial tribute.

These two years saw Moody-sponsored rallies and conferences from New York's Carnegie Hall to Royal Albert Hall in London. There were many conversions and in some instances revival. The extent of all this prompted Wilbur M. Smith to ask, "Has anyone, except a few national leaders like Abraham Lincoln, ever been so honored on the 100th anniversary of his birth?"[4]

Even as the nation still struggled to extricate itself from economic woes, the Institute broke ground for a twelve-story administration building, greatly needed to accommodate its expanding business and educational offices—then scattered in half a dozen buildings over an entire city block. It also needed additional classrooms, a larger library, and studios for radio station WMBI. Half of the money for the building came

4. Bernard R. DeRemer, *Moody Bible Institute, a Pictorial History* (Chicago: Moody, 1960), p. 80.

from Henry Crowell, who years earlier had vowed to give 60 percent of his personal income to the Lord's work.

The LaSalle Street frontage of the Moody campus changed dramatically in the late thirties. When the city had widened LaSalle Street in 1930 to accommodate increased automobile traffic, that put some of the Institute's buildings almost out in the street. One of those was the historic Auditorium, formerly Moody Church, on the corner of LaSalle and Chicago. It was finally razed in 1939—as soon as construction workers had completed the basement of Torrey-Gray Auditorium. The solution for what is today Smith Hall was not so simple. In 1939, fourteen feet had to be cut off from the front of the building, top to bottom for all eight floors!

Houghton involved himself heavily with *Moody Monthly.* By the end of the thirties, the magazine's circulation had begun to climb, with Houghton as both its editor and prime promoter. As a former actor and "creator of ideas," Houghton knew how to handle words in print.

When Will Houghton stepped into the Moody presidency, WMBI had been on the air eight years, but only sharing time with another station. These had been exciting, though chaotic, years as radio expanded across the country. Hundreds of applicants competed for air space. The government assigned frequencies one moment and canceled them the next. As stations proliferated, once clear channels found other voices crowding in.

Henry Crowell and other Institute officials made countless trips to Washington, D.C., to keep WMBI on the air. In 1934 the government established the Federal Communications Commission (FCC) to bring order out of chaos. Fortunately, in its very first year the FCC gave WMBI a good rating, in part because the station refused to offend the listening public with crass financial appeals and attacks on other religious viewpoints.

As war exploded in Europe, Houghton put radio to work in the growing world crisis. The Moody Bible Institute, he believed, should be a leader. So he initiated a chain broadcast called "Let's Go Back to the Bible," which was aired across the nation.

In 1941, WMBI began broadcasting a full day's schedule, and for the first time Moody enjoyed its own exclusive channel. It expanded into cultural and educational programming and applied for an FM license. When war restrictions on the radio industry were lifted in 1943, WMBI signed off the air at sunset, but Moody's new WDLM-FM picked up from there and broadcast until 9:00 P.M.

In the meantime, Houghton had discovered a man on the West Coast who would introduce an entirely new medium to evangelism.

In California, a young and creative minister, Irwin A. Moon, set out to show his congregation that the wonders of creation were not the result of evolution, but the work of God. To illustrate his sermons, he staged simple scientific demonstrations. The enthusiastic response prompted Moon to resign his church to give full time to this new calling. People jammed college and civic auditoriums to see and hear his "sermons from science" demonstrations.

In 1938, at the Church of the Open Door in Los Angeles, Houghton saw Moon in action and pressed him to join the extension staff of the Moody Bible Institute. At first Moon was not interested—he thought a Moody affiliation would limit his entree to the secular public. But Houghton eventually convinced him that the opposite was true.

On loan from Moody to the Christian Businessmen's Committee International, Moon proved to be one of the sensations at the San Francisco World's Fair. With more than two tons of equipment, most of it homemade, he staged a spectacle that ranged the whole field of science. Moon fried eggs on a cold stove, lighted lamp bulbs with his bare fingers, altered his voice with whiffs of a helium-oxygen mixture and unfolded a world of chemical and physical and biological wonders. As a climax he let one million volts of electricity smash harmlessly through his body.

Crowds looked and listened quietly to his insistent, thought-provoking refrain: "Can you believe these miracles are the result of chance or accident? Or are they part of a Divine Pattern? What do you think?"

With the bombing of Pearl Harbor, Moon headed off toward the warfront, not with ammunition but with the paraphernalia of a scientist. He gave live demonstrations to servicemen all over the world—and many found salvation.

But Moon knew he could reach only so many people face to face. The military, he noted, put all the training they could onto film, in order to speed the educational task. Why not put some of his own material onto film?

Moon teamed up with F. Alton Everest, former professor of electrical engineering at Oregon State University. Even evangelical Christians, they agreed, were woefully ignorant of the scientific laws that supported the very gospel message they believed.

The first film, *The God of Creation*, received rave notices in both Christian and secular reviews. Moon's time-lapse photography portrayed many facets of creation in accurate detail. These films later won awards in both the scientific and photographic world. Suddenly the Moody Institute of Science stood on the brink of a far-reaching ministry that would resound around the world.

The war years left their mark on Moody Bible Institute. Abruptly there were fewer men students than women. Graduates went off to war, a few as chaplains, and fifteen alumni gave their lives for the cause of freedom and for the gospel. The school and its related ministries forged ahead. Not even a second world war could seriously interrupt its long-standing mission. It only underscored its urgency.

As the war came to a close, Dr. Houghton brought British Lt. General Sir William G. S. Dobbie and Lady Dobbie to the United States under the auspices of Moody Bible Institute. Dobbie had distinguished himself as the heroic defender of the island of Malta, so strategically important to Allied power in the Mediterranean. He was widely known not only as a great military man but also as a devoted Christian.

During their four-month tour, the Dobbies addressed at least 150,000 people in forty cities from coast to coast, including 9,000 in Minneapolis. The ministry was aimed at middle and upper classes—those from political, business, professional, and social arenas largely unreached by the gospel message. At exclusive clubs, university gatherings, high society teas, as well as mass meetings, the Dobbies bore a unique testimony for Christ.[5]

This was the kind of creative planning in which Houghton excelled.

In Washington, D.C., the Dobbies addressed House and Senate breakfast groups and were luncheon guests of Mrs. Franklin D. Roosevelt in the White House, the President being out of the

5. Ibid., p. 93.

city. Mrs. Roosevelt was so impressed that she referred to them three different times in her nationally syndicated newspaper column.

With the war over, a climate of economic boom lay ahead. So did new frontiers for Moody Bible Institute—especially in the field of missionary aviation. But Houghton now faced a health crisis.

For thirty years he had suffered from migraine headaches, which at times had tremendously drained him. In June 1946, he experienced a heart attack. Though he temporarily recovered, he was unable to carry the heavy duties of his office. For a time he kept in close touch with the work through the dean of education, but eventually even this became impossible. Dr. Houghton died in June 1947.

The closing lines of Houghton's poem in memory of John and Betty Stam were a prayer for his own life:

In all my ways be glorified, Lord Jesus,
In all my ways guide me with Thine eye;
Just when and as Thou wilt, use me, Lord Jesus,
And then for me 'tis Christ, to live or die.

6

The Culbertson Years

Will Houghton had himself brought to the
Moody campus the man who would succeed
him. He came first as a Founder's Week speaker
in 1939, then as Dean of Education in 1942.
Newsweek magazine carried the announcement
of William Culbertson's arrival, and called him a
"large, plain, and cheerful man."[1]

Like Houghton's predecessor James M. Gray,
he was a member of the Reformed Episcopal
Church—in fact, its bishop over the New York
and Philadelphia synods. Like Gray, he was
scholarly, well educated. His convictions about
the absolute dependability of Scripture were un-
shakable. Although he refused to criticize fellow
believers for small differences in viewpoint, he
had no patience with those who did not accept

1. *Newsweek,* 1942.

the "supremacy of God's Living Word and God's Written Word."

Therefore, in no way could he support the National Council of Churches and the World Council of Churches, which he believed represented a "unity of disbelief." The further drift of these organizations even since his time has substantiated the wisdom of that position.

When the board of trustees selected Culbertson from a field of twenty-six men, he was surprised. "Very frankly," he said, "I didn't have in mind the presidency. I was content in the education field."[2]

Dr. Houghton had brought William Culbertson to Moody because he saw in him strong gifts as a Bible teacher. In his initial years at Moody, Culbertson exercised those gifts in the classroom and established a good rapport with his students, many of whom are still scattered around the globe as missionaries, pastors, and Christian leaders. Especially interested in Jewish evangelism, he made several trips to one of his favorite areas, Israel and the Middle East. Even with his multifaceted duties as president, he continued to teach one course on campus: geography of Bible lands.

From this solid base and after a year as acting president when Houghton's health failed, Culbertson stepped into the top job in 1948. Students and employees stood to greet the announcement

2. Kay Oliver, "In the Steps of D. L. Moody," *Moody Monthly*, September 1971.

with applause and the singing of the Doxology.

In some ways Dr. Culbertson stood in contrast to his predecessor. Houghton had been the promoter type. He would not hesitate, for instance, to hawk *Moody Monthly* magazine from the pulpit wherever he went. Dr. Culbertson did not feel at ease in that kind of role.

Yet the choice turned out to be right for the times. Major decisions on the school's curriculum and educational philosophy lay ahead, and that was Dr. Culbertson's forte. Neo-orthodoxy and other views of Scripture short of inerrancy surfaced in some once-conservative denominations. Culbertson held the Institute's position firm.

"As president of the Moody Bible Institute," he said in his 1966 Founder's Week message, "I want to sound again the word of warning. If we as orthodox, as evangelicals, as fundamentalists move from this doctrine [the inspiration of the Word of God], we are doomed to disaster."[3]

Although the postwar years brought a booming economy, the new president of Moody Bible Institute faced hard problems.

The GI Bill of Rights had triggered a surge of applicants, but the Institute did not have the classroom or dormitory space to accommodate them.

Salaries of faculty and employees had not kept pace with spiraling living costs. There was no

3. William Culbertson, 1966 Founder's Week message.

adequate retirement and pension plan.

The neighborhood around the campus had deteriorated. It was no longer safe to walk LaSalle Street alone. Pressures mounted for the school to move out of the city and build in the suburbs.

Some pressed that Moody Bible Institute should become a Bible college or full-fledged Christian liberal arts school. Yet the majority of the school's constituents would have protested loudly such a move.

Theological drift in segments of the church at large, though not new, worried some onlookers. Would Moody Bible Institute hold the line?

The board of trustees debated and discussed at length whether MBI should remain in the city. Thoughts of a serene campus outside the city made the option attractive. The downtown campus, strategically located, would undoubtedly bring a fine price.

But after long discussion and much prayer, the board voted to remain on LaSalle Street. The proximity of inner Chicago as a training ground and mission field could not be ignored. The city of Chicago promptly seemed to confirm the decision by vacating Institute Place, the street that jutted into the campus, and selling the whole block to Moody.

And so for the next third of a century, the Moody campus would undergo its own gigantic urban renewal program that continues today.

By 1950, a beautiful ten-story women's dormitory was rising on the corner of Chicago and

LaSalle, where the old Moody Church once stood. It was dedicated in 1951 and fittingly named Houghton Hall. That year women moved from the old 830 Building (now Smith Hall) and several small buildings into the new edifice. Men moved into the vacated 830 Building, with overflow assigned to an entire floor of the Lawson YMCA, two blocks away.

The Moody Bookstore moved from Wells Street, on the back side of the campus, to the first floor of Houghton Hall. This street-level location on the corner of one of Chicago's busiest intersections, with spacious display windows, gave the store new visibility and a well-lighted, modern atmosphere.

The basement level of Torrey-Gray Auditorium had already been completed as far back as 1939. Atop the auditorium's shallow, flat-roofed entrance on LaSalle Street stood a billboard showing how the structure would eventually appear. Gifts to the building fund, always kept separate from daily operational funds, had long been accumulating toward the completion of Torrey-Gray Auditorium. But a gift from the family of the famous gospel composer William Howard Doane, together with a sizeable bequest, suddenly expanded the plans. It would now be possible to attach a four-story music building to the rear of the auditorium, with office, classrooms, and more than seventy-five practice rooms. The Doane gift would also provide the organ for the auditorium. Work on the complex began immediately, and it was completed in time to dedicate at Founder's Week, 1955.

The year of Houghton's death in 1947, the Institute had purchased the rest of the block along Chicago Avenue, Wells Street, and Institute Place (which included sixteen stores and sixty-four apartments). The buildings were razed in 1953 to create more on-campus parking.

A campus once outdated now changed dramatically. The LaSalle Street frontage, which was what most passing motorists saw, seemed impressive. But behind this lay a mix of the old and the new. Blighted old brick buildings and apartments still huddled up against the campus on the north and west sides. The old original 153 Building sat in the middle of the crowded campus, nostalgic to many but very much in the way. It finally had to come down.

Meanwhile, the trustees approved property purchases for bookstores in other parts of Chicago and for radio stations in other cities.

Dr. Culbertson and his staff tackled the issue of Institute salaries and benefits. It could be argued that Moody Bible Institute had always been a ministry, and for the privilege of serving there one could expect to be paid somewhat less than he might earn in a secular job. But was that view fair? Even James M. Gray had hammered away at the trustees to upscale salary levels, though he never worried about himself. Many had to commute from the suburbs, adding to personal expenses.

Moody salary levels began to rise, slowly at first, but surely. Step by step, the Institute introduced improved benefits and also began to put greater stress on mid-management skills.

As the school emerged from World War II, though, more than its campus had become outdated. So also was the school's schedule. A two-year program, with only one month of break each year, did not interface well with other schools. In 1951 the Institute moved to the semester program, gave the students a full summer break, and extended the course of study to three years. This freed students to take summer jobs and to put their Moody training to work in summer camps, home mission fields, or home churches. Students could also transfer more easily into or out of other schools.

A three-year program allowed the Institute to receive college accreditation. Meanwhile, a six-week summer school drew others not regularly enrolled and kept facilities from lying idle. With the new three-year schedule came also an overhaul of curriculum.

The end of World War II brought new technology into Moody's longstanding missionary program. Sons of an evangelical pastor, Wilbur and Orville Wright had ushered in the era of flight. Now, in God's timetable, aviation would be used for the cause of the gospel.

God had used Paul Robinson, a visionary country preacher, to initiate the Moody aviation program in 1946. It soon outgrew its quonset hut facilities at Elmhurst Airport, in Chicago's western suburbs, and had to find a new home at Wood Dale Airport, just two miles from O'Hare Field.

The Missionary Technical Course put students through a major in aviation flight and mechanics but in 1954 added a second major: radio and communications. Isolated mission fields needed specialists trained in point-to-point radio communications.

Dr. Culbertson eventually had a chance to ride with Moody-trained pilots into some of the most remote pockets of the world. On a 30,000-mile worldwide tour in 1959, he sat with cannibal chiefs in New Guinea, flew to isolated mission stations in the jungles of Ecuador, and reviewed firsthand the work of Moody graduates in the heart of Africa. At Tangiers, Morocco, he met the oldest active Moody-trained missionary. H. P. Elson operated the Raymond Lull orphanage in Tangiers, but at age ninety-five (he had known Dwight Moody personally), Elson was ready to turn the work over to younger MBI graduates.[4]

Upon Culbertson's return from that world trip, the Institute stood on the brink of the sixties. And in that decade Dr. Culbertson would face his greatest challenges.

More voices were insisting that Moody become a Bible college and grant degrees. After all, were not degrees essential in the mid-twentieth cen-

4. "Inside Moody Bible Institute," *Moody Monthly*, December 1960.

tury? And no matter the actual quality of specialized education at Moody; how could a graduate without a degree convince those on the outside? To many, it seemed to make sense.

Yet was not Moody's finely-tuned emphasis on the Bible, without liberal arts accoutrements, the very thing that had set it apart from other Christian schools and helped make it great? Would not the change to a Bible college diffuse that emphasis, subtly change the campus atmosphere, spread resources too thin, and sacrifice the distinctives of its rich heritage?

In grappling with these issues, Dr. Culbertson formulated his personal philosophy of education: "Bible institutes from the time of their origin have stressed those things needed for vital Christian witness: the study of the English Bible, the winning of souls, spiritual living, missionary outreach, gospel hymnody. While certain elements have been added to the course of study, these basics remain intact. As I see it, the Bible institute is a specialized school, distinct from the liberal arts college, from the theological seminary, and from the scientific institute. Some speak of it as a religious, undergraduate, professional school."[5]

As debate swelled, Moody decided to poll its alumni. It sent out a detailed questionnaire, asked graduates to evaluate their education, and

5. Dorothy Martin, *God's Power in Action* (Chicago: Moody, 1977), p. 134.

posed the question of degrees. The replies came back: alumni regarded their education at Moody highly, but, they said, the Institute must give a degree.

Administration and faculty pondered their options. A four-year degree program, they decided, was not the answer. The uniqueness of Moody Bible Institute, decided the board, must be preserved.

The Institute announced its solution. It would continue to give diplomas to those who graduated from the three-year course. But a student who enrolled at Moody with two years of credit from an accredited liberal arts college could return for an Institute degree by taking six additional hours of Bible.

The decision preserved most of the Institute's historic curriculum, yet also changed the original course plan (which dated to the founding of the school) to a system of majors. This gave students more flexibility in choice of subjects.

William Culbertson, educator, had been largely responsible for patiently guiding the degree controversy to a wise decision.

Other ministries of Moody Bible Institute would make strides during the Culbertson era.

The Moody Institute of Science won its first international film award with its release of *City of the Bees* and caught the attention of the medical world when, for its film called *Red River of Life,* it photographed the interior valve action of the human heart for the first time. To photograph scenes for *Signposts Aloft,* Irwin Moon and associate George Speake flew a Beechcraft Bonanza (dubbed "96 Tango") around the earth, and into its nooks and crannies, covering 125,000 air miles.

In the heritage of Dwight L. Moody's Chicago World's Fair outreach, and Moon's own success decades later in San Francisco, the Moody Institute of Science reached out to further millions at world fairs in Seattle, New York, and Montreal. Some 2.5 million people went through Sermons from Science turnstiles, and hundreds of thousands of these responded to personal spiritual counsel.

Moody acquired radio stations in Cleveland, Ohio, and East Moline, Illinois, and reactivated its FM station in Chicago, boosting it to 100,000 watts in 1965.

Moody Press entered the textbook line in 1955, calling heavily upon the faculty of Moody Bible Institute to help launch the program. Their primary market: other Bible institutes, Christian colleges, and seminaries, along with pastors and laymen. Major Bible reference books, introduced in the 1960s, also helped anchor the Moody Press line—among them *The Wycliffe Bible Commentary,* produced by some forty-nine scholars from a cross-section of denominations.

The circulation of *Moody Monthly* magazine topped 100,000, establishing the magazine firmly as one of the nation's leading religious periodicals.

By the 1960s, the skies around O'Hare had become too congested, and Moody Aviation began scouring the nation for a better training base. A site in eastern Tennessee, near the base of the Smoky Mountains, seemed to stand out among others as a remarkable provision of the Lord. The newly-built but little-used modern airport at Elizabethton was far beyond what the program had earlier enjoyed. And it was in mountainous surroundings that would be much more typical of the mission field than the relative flatness of the land around Chicago. A crowd of more than one thousand, including congressmen, FAA officials, and local residents, joined MBI personnel for the Tennessee airport dedication in April 1970.

Dr. Culbertson served with other distinguished scholars on the revision committee of the Scofield Bible, a project that took many years. When he retired as Moody Bible Institute's president in 1971, he became the school's first chancellor.

Only a few days after he had conducted the inauguration of his presidential successor, George Sweeting, he entered Chicago's Swedish Covenant Hospital. He was diagnosed with cancer, a disease from which he had recovered eight years earlier.

On November 16, 1971, he met the Savior he had served so well.

7

The Sweeting Years

William Culbertson, newly appointed dean of education, walked into one of his first classes at Moody Bible Institute in 1942. In the room sat a promising young freshman from Haledon, New Jersey, who had already demonstrated his gifts for evangelism by leading high school classmates to the Lord.

Neither the professor nor the student could have guessed that twenty-nine years later, Dr. Culbertson would handpick this man to be his successor as the president of Moody Bible Institute.

For a time during his student days, the chances of an illustrious career in the Lord's service would have seemed dim to George Sweeting. At age twenty-one he became afflicted with cancer and had two major operations.

My doctor said I probably wouldn't see the year out. And even if I did, he said, "You'll never have children." My operations were followed by thirty radium treatments. My weight went down to 128 pounds.

While I was in the hospital, I said, "Lord, this bed is my altar. I want to serve You, any way You want me to serve You. I'd like to be a living sacrifice, Lord. I know You can correct physical maladies, and yet, I want Your will. I want nothing more, nothing less—nothing but the will of God."

Soon after, someone sent me a booklet on the power of God's love as a source of His power.

The first phrase of 1 Corinthians 14 says, "Follow after love. . . ." So I determined that I would pray for love, that I would cultivate the love of God in my own experience. I said, "Lord, this will be my lifetime goal."

In His mercy and grace the Lord corrected the problem. I now have four healthy sons.[1]

The girl George Sweeting would marry followed him to Moody Bible Institute. They had met during high school—on a toboggan party. "And we've been on a toboggan ride ever since," she says laughingly today.

Both were offspring of emigrants from Europe, and from Christian homes.

Sweeting's Scottish father was converted and

1. George Sweeting, "Love Is the Greatest," *Moody Monthly*, February 1982.

influenced through Bethany Hall in Glasgow, a ministry that resulted from the Moody evangelistic meetings of the late 1800s. His mother was saved in the Wishaw Baptist Church in Scotland. In 1922, they emigrated to America.

> That same year, my wife's parents arrived from Germany and settled in the same part of New Jersey. They, too, were godly people, committed to His will.
>
> During a seven-week evangelistic series, conducted in the spring of 1941 by George T. Stevens, Hilda and I sensed the Lord's working in our lives. In a special service on August 15, 1941, I felt a specific call to the Gospel ministry. After the meeting I spent time talking with the pastor about God's will for my life.
>
> Getting home meant a ten-mile bus ride and then a three-mile walk. But the ride and walk that night were special. I felt carried along by the thrill and excitement of my decision.
>
> My mother was the kind of person who never retired until all of her six children were home and in bed. That night she discerned something very important and beautiful had taken place in my life. She shared warmly about the things of God and then we knelt to pray.[2]

The Sweetings still look back on their rich days as students at Moody. Both of them "feel a great debt to the school that D. L. Moody found-

2. George Sweeting, "Thirty Five Years to the Glory of God," *Moody Monthly*, April 1976.

ed." The two were married during George's senior year.

The graduation class of 1943, to no one's surprise, chose George Sweeting as its men's speaker. At Gordon College, in Massachusetts, he graduated the president of his class. Later, Azusa Pacific College, Gordon-Conwell Divinity School, and Tennessee Temple College awarded him honorary doctorate degrees.

In the quarter century between the time George Sweeting left Moody and then returned to assume the presidency, he had left an impressive mark on the Christian scene, both at home and abroad.

For a decade as traveling evangelist and chalk artist, he spoke not only in churches and youth rallies in this country but also to thousands of servicemen on bases around the world. As head of Sweeting Crusades, his message echoed the theme "Christ Is the Answer" in many of Germany's refugee camps and in West Berlin's high schools during the post-war years.

When the oldest of his four sons became a teenager, Dr. Sweeting took the pastorate of the inner-city Madison Avenue Baptist Church of Paterson, New Jersey. He had already served two New Jersey churches early in his career, one as associate pastor of his home church—the long-respected Hawthorne Gospel Church. Five years in the heart of Paterson seasoned George Sweeting for the most challenging assignment of all:

Senior Pastor of the 4,000-seat Moody Memorial Church of Chicago.

When he accepted the call in 1967, the church, then at low ebb, had been without a pastor for three years. He would have to rebuild and also follow in the steps of men like Harry Ironside and Alan Redpath. The hard-to-reach neighborhood around the church ranged from the modern high-rise "cliff dwellers" of Sandburg Village on the church's south side to the counter culture of Old Town just two blocks west. But George Sweeting went to work on his goals and a long-range plan. Before long the church began to turn around, and attendance climbed.

Before evening services, Sweeting often mingled with the crowd, getting to know each individually. The warmth of his personality would soon penetrate to every part of the large auditorium.

"Got the joy?" he would ask, bouncing into the church office. And because enthusiasm is contagious, it soon reflected in others.[3]

It was a natural move for Moody Bible Institute to put George Sweeting on its board of trustees—as Alumni representative—once he arrived in Chicago. Then with Dr. Culbertson's approaching retirement from the presidency, the board began to look for his successor: a pastor, an

3. Kay Oliver, "In the Steps of D. L. Moody," *Moody Monthly,* September 1971.

administrator, an evangelist, an educator, one who would not forsake the heritage of Moody Bible Institute.

They found him in their very midst. Dr. Culbertson personally spoke to Sweeting about becoming president. The trustees made the request official in January 1971. Upon his installation in the fall of that same year, an event covered by all four of Chicago's major newspapers, Dr. Culbertson became the school's first chancellor.

Already Dr. Sweeting had plunged into plans for growth. A man of vision, he challenged his employees to "dream dreams" of what God might do through them and through the Institute in the years ahead. He and associates immediately went to work on a fifteen-year plan that would culminate with Moody Bible Institute's centennial in 1986.

A nationwide radio broadcast rested near the top of his priority list—one that would present the gospel and at the same time familiarize new people with the Moody Bible Institute of Chicago. He soon went on the air with a weekly half-hour program, "Moody Presents," now heard on more than 200 stations.

With the 1972 Olympics around the corner, the Institute sent fifty student counselors to Munich to join forces with the Moody Institute of Science in an outreach to the crowds. Thousands attended their daily film showings on Petershoff Square. Tragedy struck when terrorists stormed the quarters of the Israeli athletes, but even that opened unexpected doors for the gospel.

Some 262 graduates received their diplomas at the 1973 Commencement. Also honored during the ceremonies that year were the Stanley Kresges of the S. S. Kresge department store chain, whose Kresge Foundation helped provide funds to complete Houghton Hall and establish Moody Institute of Science's educational film division.

The same year, as the new inner campus and plaza emerged, Chicago Mayor Richard Daley presented MBI a Chicago Beautiful Award in recognition of "significant contributions to beautification of the City."

Late in 1973 Dr. Sweeting and the Moody Chorale retraced the steps of Dwight L. Moody through his British Isles crusades of 1873-74, exactly one hundred years earlier. In England, Scotland, and Ireland, they packed churches, school assemblies, and civic auditoriums. In 1975, music from Moody was heard from Maracaibo to Honolulu as the Concert Band toured Venezuela and the Men's Glee Club sang its way around Hawaii. In Latin America, public officials joined standing-room-only crowds.

In 1974 students and employees turned to their own Jerusalem: Chicago itself. Using the medium of direct mail, a personal letter from Dr. Sweeting went to 400,000 homes on the city's Northside. The letter outlined the plan of salvation and offered a free Moody correspondence lesson, *The Good Life.* In follow up, staff and students joined teams from thirty churches and called personally in many homes. A gigantic rally at Chicago's Medinah Temple climaxed the 1974 Chicago Evangelism Outreach (Similar campaigns reached the west and south sides of the city in 1975 and 1977).

The 1970s saw at least two great "Festivals of Praise" at off-campus locations, two at Chicago's historic, seven-tiered Auditorium Theatre and one at McCormick Place. Moody music groups also staged May noon-hour outdoor concerts in Chicago's Civic Center plaza, by arrangement with City Hall. Mayor Daley invited the Institute to enter a "religiously-themed" float in his annual Christmas parade.

A nationwide pastor's conference, also one of Dr. Sweeting's dreams, in 1973 brought to the campus more than 600 pastors from thirty-seven states, Puerto Rico, Canada, and Scotland. Only 200-300 had been anticipated. In following years attendance quickly spiraled to more than a thousand. The annual event has sent thousands of pastors back to churches with new vision, enthusiasm, and spiritual commitment.

The educational division also moved ahead. A new "Advanced Studies" program brought college graduates to the campus for thirty hours of post-baccalaureate work in an intensive one-year study. University students, often converted through one of the vigorous campus movements, took advantage of this program to ground themselves in the Scripture en route to the mission field.

Enrollment in the Evening School climbed as the Institute planted evening extension schools in places like Joliet, Illinois, and Akron, Ohio. Inner-city turmoil in the late sixties had hurt enrollment on the main campus, as people hesitated to come into the city at night. As the national mood stabilized, enrollment bounced back.

Radio also expanded in the early Sweeting years. The Institute opened WMBW in Chattanooga, then KMBI AM-FM in Spokane. WMBI-FM introduced stereo and went on a twenty-four-hour broadcasting day. Later in the decade it added two stations in Florida. In 1980, WMBI AM switched its Saturday programming to all Spanish. Chicago has an estimated one million Hispanics, and WMBI's "Radio Esperanza" reaches out to this audience.

Moody Monthly magazine more than doubled its circulation in the early '70s, climbing to one quarter-million subscribers. At a time when many religious publications declined and some even folded, the *Chicago Tribune* cited *Moody Monthly* as a striking exception. The Evangelical Press Association in 1976 named *Moody Monthly* "Periodical of the Year."

Moody Press, already with more than a thousand titles in its line, took a big step during these same years when it launched into Bible publishing, a major investment. It became a distributor of the *New American Standard Bible,* along with only four other distributors in the nation. The *Wycliffe Bible Encyclopedia,* another major project, was released in 1975. Soon to follow would be the *Ryrie Study Bible,* now Moody Press's best-selling product.

As the nation geared up to celebrate its 1976 bicentennial, so did Moody Bible Institute. Moody broadcasting developed an impressive variety of bicentennial programming. Moody Press published a colorful book, *America; God Shed His Grace on Thee,* and sent it to all members of Congress and other selected government leaders. The Institute distributed more than 100,000 colorful bicentennial calendars.

But a gigantic religious and patriotic rally in Chicago's Amphitheater on the closing Sunday afternoon of Founder's Week left the more than 12,000 who jammed the stadium with an experience they will never forget. Wesley Hartzell, reporter for the *Chicago Tribune,* called it an incredible happening in an age when the words *God* and *patriot* were being scorned.[4]

Dr. Sweeting warned that the nation was drifting disastrously away from God and the Bible, whose laws lay at the very roots of its founding.

"We of the Moody Bible Institute are not prophets of gloom and doom," he declared. "Neither are we gullible optimists."

4. Wesley Hartzell, "Bicentennial Rally Stirs Chicago," *Moody Monthly,* April 1976.

"The nation," he said, "could have no greater birthday gift than that the regular reading of the Bible be restored to the public schools."

Instead of the Bible, he observed, the nation is reading obscenity. "There are thirteen million filthy magazines sold each month. We protest them. Rome traveled this road and died. America is speeding along the same highway." Sweeting called the crowd to a new commitment to Jesus Christ, good citizenship, and godly families.[5]

The same year the Women's Glee Club and Handbell Choir toured the British Isles for a second time—Ireland, Scotland, England, Wales, then France. The next year, in 1977, Dr. Sweeting and the Moody Chorale toured Europe in a concert itinerary that took them into the Netherlands, Belgium, England, West Germany, Austria, and France. In Holland they performed live via the Dutch Television Network, and in Heidelberg, West Germany, they sang at the largest American Army Base chapel.

In 1978, when a neo-Nazi group threatened to march in the heavily-Jewish populated Chicago suburb of Skokie, Moody Bible Institute ran ads in both the *Chicago Tribune* and the *Chicago Sun-Times* outlining its support for the people of Israel and its position against the march. In the open letter, the Institute pledged to stand with the Jewish community against propaganda of hatred.

5. Ibid.

Dr. Sweeting had succeeded Irwin Moon in 1973 as the voice and figure of Moody Institute of Science, narrating the film *Empty Cities*. Filming took him into southern Mexico and the lands of the old Mayan culture. Other films like *Where the Waters Run* and *In the Beginning . . . God* followed. In 1977, Moody films released the *John Beekman Story*, documenting the extraordinary courage and impact of a Moody-trained missionary in Mexico. In the 1980s MIS added to its line films on Christian living from the pulpit of John MacArthur, Jr.

Dr. Sweeting's exposure on film worldwide strengthened his identity not only Stateside but also abroad. Periodic evangelistic missions and strategic trips to the mission fields of the world have helped to establish Moody's current president as an international figure.

In 1983, for example, Korean Christians invited him to help them celebrate the centennial of Protestant missionary influence in that land. His eight days there took him to some of Korea's largest evangelical churches, including the Young Nak Church in Seoul, which has 60,000 members, far more than any of the largest churches in America. Sweeting spoke at two of the five Sunday morning services, preaching the gospel to 30,000 people live and via closed-circuit television. That same evening, he preached at the Kwang Lim Church in Seoul, which has 12,000 members and three morning worship services. The trip culminated with a four-evening evangelistic crusade in Inchon. A thousand people made decisions to receive Christ during the crusade.[6]

As the Institute celebrates its centennial, Moody Broadcasting expands rapidly across the United States, by "translators," cable TV, and satellite. Until recently just 11 percent of the nation's population lived within the range of a Moody radio signal. Now the wonders of the space age have opened a window to all of North America.

In his wildest imaginations, Dwight L. Moody could not have foreseen the vast outreach of the school he founded. God had His hand on the life of the man Moody. And He has also prospered beyond measure the school that D. L. Moody founded. To God be the glory.

6. George Sweeting, "Land of the Morning Calm," *Moody Monthly,* September 1983.